YOUR KNOWLEDGE HAS VALUE

Bibliographic information published by the German National Library:

The German National Library lists this publication in the National Bibliography; detailed bibliographic data are available on the Internet at http://dnb.dnb.de .

Imprint:

Copyright © 2005 GRIN Verlag, Open Publishing GmbH
Print and binding: Books on Demand GmbH, Norderstedt Germany
ISBN: 9783638930154

This book at GRIN:

http://www.grin.com/en/e-book/54811/nonverbal-communication

Juliane Krueger

Nonverbal Communication

GRIN Publishing

GRIN - Your knowledge has value

Since its foundation in 1998, GRIN has specialized in publishing academic texts by students, college teachers and other academics as e-book and printed book. The website www.grin.com is an ideal platform for presenting term papers, final papers, scientific essays, dissertations and specialist books.

Visit us on the internet:

http://www.grin.com/

http://www.facebook.com/grincom

http://www.twitter.com/grin_com

Elaboration on the presentation

«Nonverbal Communication»

University of Lueneburg

Summer term 2005

Language and Communication (Sprache und Kommunikation)

Seminar: 69019 – "Conflict Talk: Sociolinguistics Meets Pragmatics"

Presented by:

Juliane Krüger

6. Semester
FB III – Applied Cultural Sciences

Deadline: 30.09.2005

TABLE OF CONTENTS

1. Introduction

Nonverbal communication accompanies us mostly unconsciously every day. We do not think what kind of gestures or distance is appropriate in certain situations. However about 60 to 65 percent of all meaning created in human encounters derives from nonverbal cues (KNAPP:246).

Studies of nonverbal communication can be traced back till times of the Roman Empire. The rhetorical treatises of Quintilian and Cicero already dealt with the meaning of hand gestures. However just in the seventeenth century with Bonifcio's and Bulwer's works gestures obtained a status "of a subject of its one right" (BULL:25). Yet elaborate study of nonverbal communication is only possible since sophisticated recording techniques have been developed which allow repeated viewing and analysis of human behaviour (for instance data gloves or video tapes). As a consequence studies of nonverbal communication developed rather lately. In the late fifties of the last century Edward HALL and Ray BIRDWHISTELL made first attempts to study nonverbal behaviour not only as a psychological function but as a means of communication. In general studies of nonverbal communication emerged as a reaction to the "overwhelming emphasis placed on verbal behaviour in the field of communication" (JONES/LEBARON:512). Subsequent a number of studies were conducted so that in the seventies nonverbal communication became an established topic (HELLER:2). In the nineties space and place received renewed interest..

This paper introduces the vast field of nonverbal communication. It is aimed at giving an overview of the different forms while focussing on proxemics, as "all behavior is located in and constructed of space"(LOW/ZÚÑIGA:1).

2. Defining nonverbal communication

There have been a variety of approaches in the study of nonverbal communication and none-theless there is no real agreement on its exact definition due to its ambiguity. There is not one single universal nonverbal language. Nonverbal communication means different things to different people and different cultures and is therefore mainly responsible for misunderstand-ings.

Generally nonverbal communication can be defined as "communicating without words through multiple communication channels" (TING-TOOMEY:200). Multiple communication channels here comprise the different media like gestures, space or time.

However there are disputes what shall be included in the term and when behaviour starts to be communication at all. One possible distinction is proposed by BURGOON/BULLER/WOODALL. They distinguish between intent, consciousness and awareness while de-fining communication (BURGOON/BULLER/WOODALL:14). WATZLAWICK and BIRDWHISTELL ar-gue that all behaviour is communication may it be intended or not: "no matter how one may try, one cannot not communicate" (WATZLAWICK:48). In contrast to that for EKMAN and FRIESEN communication is only behaviour that intends to be communicative (BULL:27). More-over in their point of view communication does not need to be shared. They argue that "communicative acts need not necessarily have a shared decoded meaning; there could be non-informative communicative acts where the sender intended to transmit a message but no one understands him" (LANE). These opponent point of views where challenged by WIE-NER. According to his viewpoint behaviour is not necessarily communicative and needs sys-tematic encoding and decoding but no intention. Communication might even take place against the intention of the encoder and without recognition of neither encoder nor decoder (BULL:27).

3. Relationship between nonverbal and verbal behaviour

"Verbal and nonverbal communication are linked together synchronously" (BIRDWHISTELL cited after CANFIELD). For a long time in research verbal and nonverbal cues where examined separately, as if they were independent phenomena. Just in the mid nineties of the last century the interrelationship between verbal and nonverbal communication attracted more and more the attention of the researchers. Since then even the terms »verbal« and »nonverbal« were criticized as being outdated, useless and misleading (JONES:500).[1]

Verbal and nonverbal communication are interrelated in certain ways. Nonverbal cues can stand alone (substitute the verbal message) or they are used together with verbal messages. Acts, that have a direct verbal translations and are used to replace words (for example when talking is difficult or impossible), are referred to as 'emblems' by EKMAN and FRIESEN (BULL:49). The so called 'ring gesture' (thumb and forefinger form a circle) or the stop gestures are examples. If nonverbal cues are used together with verbal cues they can accompany (by repeating, accenting, augmenting and illustrating) or contradict what was said verbally. For these kind of "contradictory verbal and nonverbal messages" BIRDWHISTELL coined the term 'kinesic slips' (TUBBS/MOSS:107). If such a kinesic slip occurs nonverbal cues are mostly given greater weight then what was said verbally. Moreover nonverbal messages that depict and elaborate the verbal cues are called 'Illustrators' by EKMAN and FRIESEN (BULL:49). Illustrators are used to facilitate understanding. For instance people at the hairdresser not only tell how much hair should be cut, but they will most likely show how much inches they mean by using their fingers. Illustrators can either be deictic (pointing to a location of a person, object or place) or physiographic (showing what an objects means) (BULL:49). Besides that nonverbal cues can be used together with verbal cues in order to maintain conversational coherence and/or to negotiate speaking turns. Nodding, maintaining eye contact or gestures thus function as 'turn-yielding' or 'attempt-suppressing signals' and are referred to as 'regulators' by EKMAN and FRIESEN (BULL:49). A prolonged gaze is such a signal. Before ending an utterance a speaker might look at another person signalling that he or she should take over the turn.

Comparing verbal and nonverbal messages reveals that both forms operate differently. Whereas the verbal language offers the option to refer back to what was said by using meta-communication there is no such possibility using nonverbal communication. This is crucial as potential miscommunication cannot be clarified or negotiated. Acting in order to point up "I did not mean this gesture" is not possible. If anything goes wrong in nonverbal communication people put it down to the personal level. Nonverbal cues are mainly responsible for framing first impressions by giving information about intentions and emotions. Hence people gen-

---

[1] In spite of this criticism this paper still sticks to the classification in order not to mislead the reader.

erally give greater credence to nonverbal cues when they judge style, interpret or evaluate ideas and attitudes as well as leadership qualities or credibility (TUBBS/MOSS:105). In contrast to grown-ups children however give generally more weight to verbal cues as the ability to interpret nonverbal cues just develops with a certain age.

4. Forms of nonverbal communication

Nonverbal communication is often simply equated with body language (kinesics). However it encompasses much more. It includes vocal features, facial and body movements (gaze, interpersonal distance) and even communication through smell, touch or with the help of artefacts like masks or clothes. In the following the different types of nonverbal communication are briefly described. It is intended to be rather an overview than an elaboration. Since emphasis is placed on chronemics and proxemics thereinafter.

4.1. Physical appearance

Body type, height, weight, hair, skin colour and attractiveness affect interaction between people. According to FORGAS people's physical attractiveness influences how facial cues are interpreted (TUBBS/MOSS:119). But not only the natural looks influence interaction also the way people dress and the artefacts they wear. Artefacts like jewellery, tattoos and piercings mark our identity. Physical appearance communicates age, gender, group membership, socioeconomic status and values. It reveals personality as well as culture and provides information to determine time in history (TING-TOOMEY:203;TUBBS/MOSS: 128).

4.2. Paralanguage

Besides physical appearance, paralanguage also forms identity. "Through the use of paralanguage we encode a sense of self via different nonverbal features" (TING-TOOMEY: 206). Paralanguage can be defined as the "sounds and tones we use in conversation and the speech behaviour that accompanies the message" (TING-TOOMEY:205). In short it is the way *how* something is said. By accenting different aspects of an utterance paralanguage modifies the meaning of what was said and is therefore a major source of humour, sarcasm and irony. Paralanguage is used intentionally as well as unintentionally. It can be divided in four categories: primary qualities, qualifier, differentiators and alternants. Primary qualities are timbre, volume, tempo, pitch and rhythm. These qualities are shaped by biological, physiological, psychological, social and cultural features. Qualifier are according to POYATOS "sound effects produced by several factors, from the way air is controlled in the speech organs to muscular tension and articulation as well as the anatomical configuration or speech movements of the lips, tongue, teeth and mandible"(38). Besides that paralanguage comprises differentiators like laughing, sighing, crying, coughing, yawning, sneezing, belching, shouting and whispering. Moreover "word-like single or compound sounds" (POYATOS:39) so called 'alternants' like "mmh" or "psst" are part of paralanguage and play an important role in human interaction.

Paralanguage is a potential source of misunderstanding as the meaning of different variations of certain aspects of paralanguage is shaped by cultural, ethnic and gender frames. Whereas in some cultures e.g. raising the voices is interpreted as angry in others it indicates sincerity or authenticity.

4.3. Kinesics

BIRWHISTELL'S "Introduction to Kinesics" (1952) marked the beginning of the study of kinesics. Since then a wide range of publication were devoted to "the study of posture, body movement, gestures, and facial expressions" (TING-TOOMEY:207). Kinesics consists of gestures, manners and postures. It is the field of nonverbal communication which is commonly referred to as "body language". Not included in kinesics are all movements which involve touching of another person or oneself (see haptics). Influencing factors which shape the communicative content of gestures by altering the intensity, range and speed of a movement are age, status, sex and culture.

One offshoot of the study of kinesics which should be looked at in detail in the following is the study of synchrony. People's movement is innately attuned to their words. Movements of all parts of the body are related to vocal stress, syntax and meaning. Changing a standpoint leads to changing posture. This characteristic is called `self synchrony` by CONDON and OGSTON (BULL:47). Being "in sync" is a form of communication itself. Children synchronize their movement to speech from the first days onwards (HALL 1989:73). Furthermore people not only synchronize their own words and behaviour, but also attune to the movements of their interlocutor. This interactional synchrony takes places on the vocal and the nonverbal level and even in terms of body functions. As experiments with electroencephalographs revealed people in conversation not only accustom their position and body movements but even their brains (HALL 1989:73). Synchronic behaviour illuminates also dominance relations. The nondominant partner in general follows the rhythmic pattern of the dominant one, but disengaging is possible through establishing one's own rhythmic pattern (for instance by changing the tone). However interfacing is only possible when interlocutors synchronize their rhythmic pattern. As humans can only deal with one rhythm at one time "rhythmic interactional synchrony is precondition for successful communication" (RAFFLER-ENGEL:89). Body rhythms which differ radically lead to conflict. Common sayings like "being on the same wavelength" or to "tune in" suggest the importance of synchrony. But in spite of the relevance of synchrony people are hardly aware of it. Due to the lack of consciousness dyssynchronic behaviour is not identified and according to RAFFLER-ENGEL (89) "the most serious [and enduring] problem in cross-culture communication." It does not only lead to misunderstanding but to mistrust, which is much harder to overcome. The reason of this conflict is rooted in the pressure of conforming one's own body rhythm to another's body rhythm, which marks an extreme invasion of privacy and may even lead to a total collapse of communication.

4.4. Haptics

Haptics "examine the perception and meaning of touch behaviour" (TING-TOOMEY:212). Touching is a bonding gesture and essential for psychological and physical well-being. Intimacy, sociability and connectivity are expressed by touching. Touching pattern change according to the degree of familiarity, status and the communicative context. As relationships become more intimate mutual gazes and touch frequency increase, while in interpersonal distance decreases. Different cultures adhere to different touching rules. Public display of affection, better known as 'PDA', varies highly across cultures. Whereas in Islamic cultures same-sex touching is regarded as normal and has nothing to do with sexual interest, the same behaviour might be interpreted differently in America or Germany. Researchers distinguish between high, moderate and low contact cultures. High contact cultures prefer direct eye contact, face each other, touch and kiss frequently and speak in a rather loud voice. Examples are countries like France, Italy, Russia and Latin America. Low contact cultures like the Chinese or Japanese use little touching, prefer indirect eye gazes and speak in lower tone. Our society could be classified as a moderate contact culture like USA, Canada and Australia. Germans show patterns of both classifications and in general rather discourage touching except for intimate situations (Tubbs/Moss:111-112).

4.5. Oculesics olfactics and chromatics

Elaborating on nonverbal communication one also has to mention further forms. Eye contact is one of the most important communicative forms among facial expressions. "The study of the role of eye behaviour such as eye contact, eye movements and pupils dilation in communication is called oculesics" (TUBBS/MOSS:107). Eye contact reveals personality, true emotion and intention as it is a spontaneous response which can not be controlled. Apart from the eyes 'olfactics' the "study of the sense of smell" (IC), is part of nonverbal communication. One's culture and sex influence the perception of odours. Smell is a means of forming identity and orientation (landscapes of smell, smell linked memories). In Arab countries while establishing and maintaining contact olfactics are actively involved. In contrast to Americans and Europeans Arab people rather stay inside the olfactics bubble of their interlocutor (Hall 2003:63). Furthermore smell can be used as a principle method of organizing time. The Andaman Islanders for example have constructed their calendar on the basis of odours by naming the different periods of the year after the fragrant flowers that bloom at that time (IC). Chromatics deals with the way how colours communicate. Colours are thought to influence behaviour and moods. However the study of colour and its influence on human behaviour is only beginning to receive research attention, still popular notions seem to be predominant.

4.6. Chronemics

The term chronemics is defined as "how human beings communicate through their use of time" (TUBBS/MOSS:113). People say time is saved, spent, wasted, made up, slowed down or running out. These expressions expose our perception of time. Everything we do is interwoven with time. Time is conceived as an tacit determinant or frame on which everything else is built on (HALL 1989:19). Humans are hardly aware how their social and business life is shaped according to their concept of time. Hall states: time "influences subtly in depth how we think"(HALL 1989:21). The prevailing patterns of time designate when one should eat, work, sleep or play. Life stages and religion are closely related to the sense of time (TING-TOOMEY:113). When one does something is of importance and even shapes the meaning of what one is doing. A call in the morning or late at night is interpreted differently than a call at daytime. "All cultures organize themselves around their conceptions of time" (HAMPDEN-TURNER:295). Through and over time cultures reveal themselves. Time patterns differ not only between cultures but even between regions, families, men, women and members of different status or occupation. Nevertheless people are hardly aware of their own timeframe. Just in contact with other cultures - who treat time differently – they realize the meaning of time. Concepts of time which seem to be totally natural for one's own culture are artificial for other cultures. Tiv living in Nigeria the week is a totally strange and unnatural period. For them time is seen as a capsule. There is a certain time for certain things (like working, fishing, visiting) during which they are just doing these things (HALL 1990:16). Moreover there are even cultures which do not know the meaning of time at all. As for the Hopi time is not a quantity and not measurable at all (HALL 1990:173) and the Sioux have no words for late and waiting and therefore do not know what these terms mean (HALL 1990:13).

All in all two different time patterns who govern cultures and effect the very core of existence are distinguished by HALL (1989:24). First of all there is the monochronic time pattern. This time concept regards time as being segmented and linear (TUBBS/MOSS:115). Thus it is also called linear-active model. Time is seen as a road, it flows fast - past time is over, but the present one can control, arrange and make it work for oneself. Cultures which use this time concept value clock time and schedules a lot. Deviating from the agenda, changing schedules and appointments is despised. Wasting time is demonised as time is money and hence efficiency is important. Following people living according to that concept usually do one thing at a time. On average one is rather future focused and task oriented. Countries which are well known for their use of the monochronic time system are individualistic countries like United States, Germany, Switzerland, Austria, Netherlands, United Kingdom and Scandinavia. The second main concept of time is called polychronic or multi-active time. This time concept regards time as a point. Time is "experientially based" and situational (TING-TOOMEY:224). People living up to this concept are not interested in schedules or punctuality but give priority to the completion human transaction and events (TING-TOOMEY:223). There is always time to chat and meet people and therefore the saying "my time is up" is just used if death is coming. Moreover simultaneous activities prevail. Cultures which stick to this concept are rather past and present-focused, but do not care about future times. Predominantly Arab, African, Mediterranean and collective cultures in general make use of this time concept. According to HALL these two time patterns are polar opposites (TING-TOOMEY:222). Interaction of people belonging to different time patterns might cause conflicts especially in the working world. For instance monochronic time dominates do not see the large whole due to compartmentalization of time and think of people of the other system as being lazy and unproductive.

In addition to this two time pattern there is the so called cyclic and the unfolding time. Cyclic time is neither linear nor event or personality related. It is not racing away but coming up again in circles, so that the past is always there in the present. Cyclic time oriented people are not that disciplined in their planning as they believe that time can not be managed but is harmonized with the cyclic laws of nature. This time concept prevails in Asian countries (HAMPDEN-TURNER:57). Japanese people however have a different time concept. In their sense of unfolding time Asian indirectness and the importance of rituals for the Japanese society are reflected. Japanese segment time a lot and like to know all the time where they stand in relation to the whole. Each event (birthday, tea ceremony or even the cleaning of the house) is broken up in various phase with marked beginning and ending. Small gestures like the exchange of business cards serve as a marker of the beginning of such a ceremony (HAMPDEN-TURNER:60-61).

4.7. Proxemics

The term proxemics, denoting "the study of how human beings communicate through their use of space" (TUBBS/MOSS:109), was coined by E.T. HALL an anthropologist studying how culture influences spatial behaviour and perception .The two systems - time and space - are functionally interrelated (HALL 1989:17). Time unfolds in space and vice versa. Not only time but also space transmits meaning to the people surrounding us. According to HALL "thousand of experiences teach us, that space communicates" (1990:161). Privacy, home, boundaries, furniture arrangement and propinquity are just some aspects of the vast field of proxemics.

Digression: Methodology

Space is studied mainly by observation. Major tools for the study of proxemics are photographs and videotapes, which offer the possibility to check observation. Moreover comments which people make, when spatial etiquette is violated are a source of data- for instance "I wish he would stop breathing down my neck. I can't stand that" (HALL 2003:57). Literature and art are also cultural data which reveal spatial patterns (HALL 2003:60). Besides that there are experiments which reveal people's proxemics patters. By simply asking people to arrange objects so that they are "close", "far away" or "together" one can distinguish cultural differences in spatial treatment (HALL 2003:57).

"Space is socially constructed" (PELLOW:160, LOW/ZÚÑIGA:15) and develops through practice (LOW/ZÚÑIGA:10). People transform general and indefinite space into meaningful places by social exchanges, images, memories and their daily use of infrastructure. Places are "politicized, culturally relative, historically specific, local and multiple constructions" (RODMAN:203) which indicate social organisation, religion, economic system and culture in general.

Humans are 'territorial animals', everyday people claim space, built on it and in this way mark their territory (HALL 1989:159; PELLOW:160). Entering a classroom students feel uncomfortable not being able to sit on "their" chair. The well-known territory, even just the position of a chair, makes people feel comfortable and secure. If somebody invades one's territory by taking the regular seat one feels vulnerable and it is a threatening experience. This feeling is a remnant of an old era. As in the past humans had to defend their territory in order to survive (TING-TOOMEY:214). Although people are anchored in space and have developed a strong sense for territory, at large nobody speaks about the importance of space and people are even unable to express how they set distances. "Nobody is taught to consider space secluded from other associations. Feelings cued by the handling of space are often attributed to something else" (HALL 1990:161). Just when people's own concept of space is challenged, for example when people travel they realize the importance of space in everyday life.

The space surrounding ourself is dynamic and can be divided in different zones, which only exist in relation to others. HEDIGER first described personal and social distance in operational terms (Hall 2003:54). Following HALL developed his spatial classification system. He distinguishes four different spatial zones: intimate, personal, social and public zone. The closest surrounding is the intimate space (0 - 45 cm), which lends itself mainly for nonverbal communication with family and close friends. It is considered improper for public places. The adjacent distance is the personal distance (45 cm - 1,2 m), which can be defined as "the bubble that an organism maintains between itself and others" (HALL 1989:119) in order "to be able to think, talk and gesture in comfort" (LEWIS:132). Personal space depends on personality, communication style and culture. Next to these mere personal zones there is the social distance (1,2m - 3,6m) - which is suitable for gatherings and business meetings - and the public distance (3,6 m and more). Operating in public distance asks for louder voice, more formal style of language and reduced speech rate.

Not only that these zones are changing dynamically but also human's perception of space is dynamic. It is rather formed by the activities they perform in a certain space and not by what they see or feel (PELLOW:162). Moreover space itself derives its meaning from practice (LOW/ZÚÑIGA:10).The bubble of space in which one moves and feels comfortable changes dynamically subject to those around us, our feelings and the topic of a conversation.

Japanese attitude towards personal space is an example of this dynamic adaptation process of personal space. In non crowded situations Japanese need of personal space is even greater than the American one. However in forced crowds like on busses or on a train Japanese do not avoid frequent body contact even with strangers. Similarly personal space is very close among friends and family. This behaviour expresses the collectivist orientation of the Japanese. In un-crowded situation space functions as a "barrier against the unknown" (SAMOVAR:259), thus in forced crowds Japanese will ignore the awkward closeness with a "façade of imperturbable passivity" in order to maintain harmony (SAMOVAR:259).

People who communicate, constantly negotiate the personal space between them. While communication different personal distances lead to a kind of "dance" as the interlocutors try to adapt to unfamiliar personal space by backing up or moving forward in order to feel comfortable. At critical stages in life humans need "specific amounts of space in order to act out the dialogues that lead to the consummation of most of the important acts in life." (HALL 2003:54). If people are forced to communicate in an unfamiliar distance, communication can be difficult which may lead to what GOFFMAN calls 'alienation in encounters' (HALL 2003:57).

"Spatial changes give a tone to a communication, accent it, and at time even override the spoken word" (HALL 1990:175).

Our sense of distance and space is rooted in culture. Wherever people go they carry their own concept of space with them. "There is no fixed distance-sensing mechanism [...] in man that is universal for all cultures" (HALL 2003:63). Growing up people learn many different spatial cues, each having several meanings depending on the context. Thus a child requires five to six years to master the basic concepts of space (HALL:1989:164). As grown-ups in their own culture people automatically adjust to the proper distance and interpret spatial cues according to the prevailing rules. Travelling people experience sensitively differences in handling space. In the intercultural context the spatial treatment can be fixed, sem-fixed or dynamic (HALL 2003:61). Walls and boundaries are rather treated as fixed features, whereas territory could be semi-fixed or even dynamic for instance in the nomadic context. Another example of spatial features that are seen as fixed or semi-fixed is furniture. If one person considers certain things as fixed and others do not these differences in spatial treatment can cause anger and anxiety (HALL 2003:61). Analogous to haptics the concept of high and low-contact cultures can be applied to proxemics. People from high-contact cultures use less personal space compared to people from low contact cultures. For example whereas the average personal distance for Europeans or Americans is 20 inches, for Arab it is only 9 to 10 inches (TING-TOOMEY 2005:215). And even in a smaller scale these differences are perceivable: people from North Europe require more distance than people from the south of Europe.

Our system of space treats space in terms of a co-ordinate system and utilizes the edges of things. A different spatial organisation is the one used by the Hopis: They do not conceive space as points and lines like we do, they do not have terms for intern three dimensional spaces like room, hall, cellar as these spaces are not named but rather located (HALL 1990:169). These different spatial patterns may lead to misunderstanding, anger, aggression, and conflict in the intercultural context. Spatial differences are primarily responsible for the so called culture shock (HALL 1990:170). Being in another country therefore calls for learning the system of space in order to prevent these misunderstandings. Language learning is the first step to do so, as researchers have shown that speaking a different language people automatically approximate the distance norm of the culture of which they speak the language (TUBBS/MOSS:113).

Not just distance between people, but also the environment has a strong influence on a persons behaviour. Behaviour is, as said before, defined by the person interacting and the environment in which communication takes place. To illustrate this relation LEWIN uses the formula $B = f(P,E)$ [B= Behaviour, E= Environment, P= Person] (TING-TOOMEY 2005:217). This relationship can also be described by the term »inscribed space« which focuses on the questions how meaning is attached to space, how space is transformed in place and how space provokes memories (LOW/ZÚÑIGA:13).

Peoples' home territory or immediate environment has a strong influence on their (daily) life and on themselves as people incorporate qualities of their environment (HALL 2003:53, FER-NANDEZ:187). Houses for instance communicate as well. Through their physicality houses operate "as a complex idiom for defining social groupings, naturalizing social positions, and as a source of symbolic power" (CARSTEN and HUGH-JONES city after LOW/ZÚÑIGA:12) Comparing different types of middle class houses for example the American and the Mexican illustrates cultural differences. Being rather physically separated by fences, gates, yard and lawn American houses represent the individualistic society. Mexican houses are integrated in a plaza, with a community center inside, which offers plenty of space to meet friends or other people. Analogues different cultural groups have different expectation regarding the room functions. In general the house is the gendered space which is most frequently recognized (LOW/ZÚÑIGA:8). This is especially obvious in Arab cultures with their separate sections for males and females (TING-TOOMEY 2005:217). Studying the Algerian houses BOURDIEU points out, that houses are physically and conceptually divided in male and female parts. Linking women to the lower, dark and hidden and men to the light, warm and upper parts (BOURDIEU after LOW/ZÚÑIGA:8-9.) Studying the houses in Ghana DEBORAH PELLOW highlights that women's subordination to men is rooted in their primary association with the domestic sphere (PELLOW:162).

Space and its handling signals priorities, importance and status - "organizing, meaning and use of space express hierarchy of social structural relationships and ideologies encoded in it" (ARDENES cited after LOW/ZÚÑIGA:9). This is in particular meaningful in the working world. Considering the impact of environment in the context of work reveals that e.g. working surroundings have a strong and even debilitating effect on workers performance (HALL 1989:19). The amount of space people use and the place where a worker is seated in a company communicate a lot about the relationship to the organization and the relevance of the worker. Cross-culturally there are examples for certain differences in office-arrangements and their effect on power and social relations (HALL 1990:171). If a new person starts working in an office in the US the whole office will be rearranged and in this way the presence of a new worker is acknowledged. Everybody moves in order to share the space, as in the American cultural frame the given space is to be divided equally. Besides that the center in an American office room is reserved for the group. Contrary to that in France space is not shared with new colleagues and the leading character is sitting in the middle of the office controlling and observing everything (HALL 1990:171).

5. Communicating emotions – Black and White styles in conflict[*]

Nonverbal cues are particular important in the communication of emotions. People rely on nonverbal aspects of communication when interpreting emotional states, intentions and feelings. Studying emotional expression has a long history. Rather lately however the perception of emotion and how expression induce emotions are studied.

Concerning the development of emotional expression there are two point of views: the universal versus the culture relativistic perspective. CHARLES DARWIN is a representative of the universalistic approach. By asking people to identify certain emotions from still photographs, he tried to find out whether certain emotions are universal or not. In his point of view facial expression of emotion are »instinctive« (TUBBS/MOSS:118) or in other words an "universal and constitute part of an innate, adaptive, physiological response" (BULL:29). On the other hand there is the culture relativistic perspective, which is represented by BIRDWHISTELL. He contradicts CHARLES DARWIN'S point of view arguing that the display of emotions is learned and thus cultural specific (BULL:29). These two opposed views were united by EKMAN'S neurocultural model which states that facial expression of emotion are innate and learned. Evidence for the innateness of emotion derives from the universality of seven facial expressions (sadness, anger, disgust, fear, interest, surprise, and happiness) – SADFISH which have be recognized in cross-cultural experiments by showing photographs coining these expressions to people from various cultures (TUBBS/MOSS:119).[2] Basically these universal expressions are inborn but adapted through learning. There are cultural specific modifications and definite rules when, to whom and how emotions are revealed - so called »display rules« which are learned from the environment from the first days of life. Different display rules are especially obvious between individualistic and collectivistic cultures. In individualistic countries it is acceptable to express emotions like anger or disgust whereas in collectivistic cultures anger and disgust are in general not expressed in public in order to preserve harmony (TING-TOOMEY 2005:208).

Another striking example of different emotional display is the 'black' cultural group. Blacks and Whites operate according to different cultural conventions and thus show different modes of behaviour and emotional display. According to HALL Blacks use different forms of nonverbal cues which are more subtle than the white one's. Experiences with lower class black communities revealed that theses cues are almost imperceptible to Whites (HALL 2003:57). Similar KOCHMAN points out, that there are conflicts due to the different verbal and

---

[*] In the following the terms "Blacks" and "White" are used a categorization and are not meant to be racist or discriminate.
[2] Due to the fact that controlled and spontaneous emotions are detected differently (spontaneous are much more difficult to detect) experience which just make use of still photographs to study emotions are only partly reliable (TUBBS/MOSS:119).

nonverbal communication modes of Blacks and Whites. In the following the different display rules of these two cultural groups are presented.

Blacks are a high-contact culture. They make greater use of their body and speak in a louder voice. The black behavioural mode is high-keyed which means animated, interpersonal and confrontational (KOCHMAN:18). Emotions play a functional role in Blacks activities in order to harmonize the intern and the extern. Thus they favour forceful spontaneous expressions and freedom of self-assertion and regard more subdued restraint expression as cold and false (KOCHMAN:107). Rhythm is of great importance in black movements. Talking, walking (bopping), dancing, worshipping – everything is done in a certain rhythm. Moreover in black cultural patterns people's own style is of great importance. Everything is a performance (KOCHMAN:131-134).

Contrary white behaviour is according to KOCHMAN low-keyed meaning "dispassionate, impersonal and non-challenging" (KOCHMAN:18). Whites value the ability to rein their impulses and hence practice self-control (KOCHMAN:113). They are ruled by norm and not by the force of their feelings. Spontaneous expression –"showing off"- or individual self-assertion are devalued. Emotional behaviour is regarded as threatening and unintelligible as Whites have hardly capacity for letting go emotions. Due to this behaviour Whites are labelled as "gray"- lifeless, boring, conformist and unimpassioned by Blacks (KOCHMAN:107).

These different modes of behaviour are causing tension, anger and conflicts in intercultural encounters and especially when it comes to solving arguments. While arguing Blacks "present their views as advocates. They take a position and show that they care about this position" (KOCHMAN:20). They also expect others to challenge these views and to engage in persuasive argument that will lead to further clarification and truth. Overall they are personally much more involved which can easily be misunderstood in the white cultural frame. Since Whites tend to present their views as observers, using the "relatively detached and unemotional discussion mode to engage an issue" (KOCHMAN:106).

These differences reveal the importance of competent knowledge of the different forms of nonverbal communication in certain cultures in order to prevent misunderstanding and conflict.

6. Synopsis

Nonverbal communication is constantly present in human interaction and conveys a significant percentage of social meaning. Verbal and nonverbal messages are interrelated and therefore cannot be studied separately.

There is no universal nonverbal language. Nonverbal communication is rooted in culture and thus culturally specific. Culture and the social system form and transform nonverbal communication and in this way make it complex and ambiguous. Analogues to culture and its richness of forms there is an abundance of forms of nonverbal communication. By giving an overview of the different forms of nonverbal communication this paper illustrated this vast field which comprises much more than what is commonly equated with body language.

Space is an essential component of sociocultural theory and both cultural and social systems are grounded in space. It is the nonverbal variable that influences people's behavior in depth but is seldom addressed or talked over in daily life. Hence it received special attention and was looked at in more detail in this work.

Being in another culture asks for learning their system of nonverbal communication in order to prevent miscommunication. By elaborating on the differences of Black and White communicational forms, cultural display rules and the significance of nonverbal cues as an important means of communicating emotions were revealed in this paper.

7. Literature

BULL, P.: <u>Communication under the Microscope. The Theory and Practice of Microanalysis</u>. London: Routledge, 2001.

BURGOON, J. K. /BULLER, D. B./ WOODALL, W. G.: <u>Nonverbal communication: The unspoken dialogue</u>. New York: Harper & Row, 1989.

CANFIELD, A.: <u>Body, Identity and Interaction: Interpreting Nonverbal Communication</u>. Etext.net: Custom Electronic Text Publisher 2002, URL: http://canfield.etext.net/.

FERNANDEZ, J.: <u>Emergence and Convergence in some Afrian Sacred Places.</u> In: Low, S.M./ Lawrence-Zúñiga, D.: The anthropology of space and place: Locating culture. Oxford: Blackwell, 2003, p. 187-204.

HALL, E.T.: <u>Beyond culture</u>. New York: Doubleday, 1989.

HALL, E.T. :<u>The silent language.</u> New York: Doubleday, 1990.

HALL, E.T.: <u>Proxemics.</u> In: Low, S.M./ Lawrence-Zúñiga, D.: The anthropology of space and place: Locating culture. Oxford: Blackwell, 2003, p. 51-74.

HAMPDEN-TURNER, C.M. / TROMPENAARS, F.: <u>Building Cross-Cultural Competence. How to create wealth from conflicting values.</u> Chichester: John Wiley & Sons, 2000.

HELLER, M. C.: <u>Introducing Postural Dynamics</u>, 2005, URL: http://www.aqualide.com/ up-load/texte/text30.pdf.

JONES, S.E../LEBARON C.D.: <u>Research on the Relationship Between Verbal and Nonverbal Communication: Emerging Integrations</u>, Journal of Communication,Vol. 52 (2002), 3, p. 499-521.

KOCHMAN, T.: <u>Black and white: Styles in conflict</u>. Chicago: University of Chicago Press, 1981.

KNAPP, M./ DALY, J.A.: <u>Handbook of Interpersonal Communication</u>. Thousand Oaks: Sage Publications, 2002.

LANE, D. R.: <u>Function and Impact of Nonverbal Communication in a Computer Mediated Communication Context: An Investigation of Defining Issues</u>, URL: http://www.uky.edu/~drlane/techno/nvcmc.htm.

LEWIS, R.: <u>When Cultures Collide. Managing successfully across cultures</u>. London: Nicholas Brealey Publishing, 1996.

Low, S.M./ LAWRENCE-ZÚÑIGA, D.: <u>Locating Culture.</u> In: Low, S.M./ Lawrence-Zúñiga, D.: The anthropology of space and place: Locating culture. Oxford: Blackwell, 2003, p.1-48.

MARTIN, J. N.: <u>Intercultural communication in contexts</u>. Boston: McGraw-Hill, 2004.

MASIP, J.: <u>Nonverbal Communication. Nonverbal Behavior links</u>, 2003, URL : http://www3.usal.es/~nonverbal/introduction.htm.

PELLOW, D.: The Architectur of female Seclusion. In: Low, S.M./ Lawrence-Zúñiga, D.: The anthropology of space and place: Locating culture. Oxford: Blackwell, 2003, p. 160-185.

POYATOS, F.: Cross-Cultural Perspectives in Nonverbal Communication. Toronto: C.J. Hogrefe, 1988.

RAFFLER-ENGEL, W. (1988): The impact of covert factors in cross-cultural communication. In: Poyotas, F.: Cross-Cultural Perspectives in Nonverbal Communication. Toronto: C.J. Hogrefe, 1988, p. 71-106.

RODMAN, M.C.:Empowering place:Multicoality and Mutlivocality. In: Low, S.M./ Lawrence-Zúñiga, D.: The anthropology of space and place: Locating culture. Oxford: Blackwell, 2003, p. 204-224.

SAMOVAR, L.A./ PORTER, R. E. : Intercultural Communication. A reader. Belmont: Wadsworth Publishing, 1997.

SCOLLON, R./ SCOLLON, S.W.: Intercultural Communication. Oxford: Blackwell, 2001.

TING-TOOMEY, S. /CHUNG, L.C.: Understanding Intercultural Communication. L.A.: Roxbury Publishing, 2005.

TUBBS, S.L./ MOSS, S.: Human Communication: Principles and Context. Boston:McGraw-Hill, 2003.

WATZLAWICK, P./ BEAVIN, J.H./ JACKSON, D.D.: Menschliche Kommunikation, Bern:Huber, 1990.

AUTHOR NOT STATED:

(IC) Intercultural Communication, URL :
        http://www.saintmarys.edu/~berdayes/vincehome/courses/comm350/comm350.html.

YOUR KNOWLEDGE HAS VALUE

- We will publish your bachelor's and
  master's thesis, essays and papers

- Your own eBook and book -
  sold worldwide in all relevant shops

- Earn money with each sale

Upload your text at www.GRIN.com
and publish for free